Our Lands Are Not So Different

Our Lands Are Not So Different

Michael Bazzett

HORSETHIEF BOOKS

© 2017 Michael Bazzett
All Rights Reserved
Printed in the United States

Exterior Design: Andrew Shuta
Interior Design: Jakob Vala

Library of Congress Cataloging-in-Publication Data

Bazzett, Michael
[Poems. Selections.]
Our Lands Are Not So Different/ Michael Bazzett
Pages; Cm
ISBN: 978-0-9982463-1-4 (hardcover)
LCCN: 2016958904

First Printing

HORSETHIEF BOOKS LLC
P.O. Box 1661
Iowa City, IA 52245-1661

www.horsethiefbooks.com

For Leslie

Contents

I.

Our Lands Are Not So Different · 1

Verisimilitude · 4

The Party · 6

The Book · 8

Nine Possible Observations to Consider · 10

Crow · 12

The Date · 14

Thought Grenade · 16

from The Book of Time · 17

Wind · 20

The Problem of Measurement · 22

She · 24

In the Capital · 26

The Differences · 27

The Choice · 29

The Buzzard and Reversal · 30

Coming Home · 32

Solitude · 34

Rooms and Days · 38

Animal · 40

The Mind Forest · 41

Man · 43

II.

At the Café · 47

The Room · 48

The Anecdotalist · 50

The Taxidermist and The Cloud · 53

In The Land of My Fathers · 55

The Doppelgängster · 57

There Is Nothing · 59

The Weight of a Shadow · 61

The Ottoman · 62

The Woman · 63

The Delicate Skull of a Small Animal · 64

Stephen · 65

Humbleman · 67

Hedgehog · 69

The One-Time Monster · 71

The Important Book · 72

Change · 74

When He Lay Down Beneath the Earth · 77

III.

Afterward · 81

The Operation · 83

The Nineteenth Century · 85

Unhinged · 88

Things No One Expected to Be True
Until Viewing the Film · 91

Orpheus and Eurydice · 94

Her Wrath · 95

Parable · 99

Report from Beyond · 100

The Invisible Book · 102

The Dinner Party · 104

Other People · 106

The Shadow · 108

The Goat · 109

The Limb · 110

History · 112

Wrecked · 114

Excavation · 115

Chain Store · 117

The Sentence · 118

Odds · 119

Breathless · 121

Hair · 123

June · 125

Acknowledgements · 129

I.

Our Lands Are Not So Different

When I first arrived on your shores
I was young and a little foolish and looked
to arrange certain elements of my clothing
so that I would be mistaken as a native
when riding the morning train to my studies—

I felt the key was finding the right shoes
as well as an air of easy belonging
yet my nonchalance was as put on
as the newly acquired knot I used to tie my scarf

(Perhaps you remember the one?

A clever arrangement from some years back
where the muffler is looped once around the neck
then pulled down taut across the genitals
and drawn snugly up through the buttock
cleft so that a belt is rendered unnecessary)

The train would rock through every curve
and I would sway on the bench and secretly admire
the leather harnesses you use with wayward children
as well as the arousing way your older women
often touched me in the marketplace

Perhaps I should also admit
the fact that you encourage your children
to play piano without wearing mittens
strikes me as laughable even to this day—

especially when I consider the pride my parents felt
at hearing my flipper-like hands bash the keys
the sense memory of wool sliding on ivory
and the rippling ease with which nocturnes fell
from naked fingers once released—

Yet these are differences I now see
as superficial, much like a laminated film
wrapping the bodies of fraternal twins

and given our mutual language

it seems quite possible that you are thinking

the same thoughts as I am upon reading these words—

So why not come for a visit?

There is little doubt that you will feel at home

Just be certain to bring your book of laws

and the cowhide helmet sewn with boar's teeth—

Once you check in with the Central Registry

to read the dossier that has been compiled

to determine exactly who it is that you think you are

then the rest is easy: just be yourself—

Verisimilitude

After he lost his post at the university,
the philosopher began making very short films.
In one, two men stared fixedly at a chess board.
As one contemplates his move, the other slowly raises
a revolver until it is level with his opponent's chest.
In another, a woman is tumbling out of her
opened blouse. Two construction workers
jackhammer the street behind her, kicking
a shuddering cloud of white dust into the air.

A newborn child approaches behind the wheel
of an expensive sedan, heavy with chrome. This
is too easy, says the woman, with an air of finality.
In one film, everything is on fire, including the fire.
The tiny fire that burns the fire itself is clearly
the real attraction and the normal fire looks
clumsy and disheveled by comparison.

In the last film, a disrobed man sits on a thin sheet
of paper laid across a sturdy vinyl-covered bench.
He is examining the paper as he sits there alone
and you can almost hear him thinking this
paper doesn't provide much of a barrier against
what ails him, when a doctor interrupts his reverie
and says, "Prolapsed uterus is the only thing we can
rule out with any certainty," and then reaches for
two purple gloves from a dispenser on the wall
and rummages through a cabinet until he finds
a Ziploc bag holding a grimy roll of dollar bills.
"Here," he says thrusting it toward the man,
"you'll no doubt need this wherever you're going."

The Party

She stood in the kitchen talking to a man
who specialized in enslaving the wind.

"We inject dye into it so it's easily captured," he said,
leaning against the counter. Even strong winds
are docile once caged. I mean,

at the end of the day it's just air, right? "We
could put a hurricane in that oven right now,"

he murmured, motioning toward the brushed
stainless appliance with his drink. She nodded

politely, trying to continue with her line of
questioning, but it had gone utterly slack.
There was no place to tether the line—

the cupboards, maybe?—plus it was clearly
impossible to concentrate with that slave
master droning on and on, so what she did was
start repeating back the last three words of

every phrase he uttered and now he is in love.

The Book

This relationship is as promising as any you've encountered
after a dozen words—so before we go further let's make it clear
that a number of us are invested in this: a handful of you
as well as a number of them and god knows how many of me,

and then there is the book itself, a physical artifact made
from the pressed fibers of myriad trees which breathed
carbon dioxide generated by untold thousands of exhalations
some of which may well have been made by one *you*, singular,
giving you a stake in this similar to that of the male eelpout
who jets his cloudy milt over a writhing mob of females
and then swims on. No fingerling will ever call him *Daddy*.

In fact, there is not a word for it in the eelpout lexicon,
which admittedly is rather limited, and one of the primary reasons
we have decided to compose this in English. The ink of this book
is called bone-black because it is made from charred femurs
and ribs trucked from the abattoir, a word I have always found
unnervingly lovely in my mouth even though it is impossible
to find a definition of it that doesn't employ the word *slaughter*.

Following this etymological line would lead us all into a real
shambles, which means "disorganized failure, messy disorder, place
of carnage." And it gets grimmer when we arrive at definition
number four: "Same as slaughterhouse." Ink and paper
are not simple, and we have yet to even mention the one-winged
bird and how she hops, so spry, and how the song she sings
uses only half the notes and thus never flutters far from the ground.
And how the cat's slinking shadow

                                    comes, drawn by the sound—

Nine Possible Observations to Consider

1. The sound a bluejay makes, if it were a color, would not be blue. It would be the color of something torn open.

2. The ubiquity of dust.

3. Two men enter a room. One asserts time is an invention, the other claims it as a discovery. They stare into one another's eyes. The exact length of this pause has yet to be determined.

4. Roughly half of all food is discarded, leading observers to conclude that we could, if necessary, live on the moon.

5. It is a truth universally acknowledged that absolutes are not to be trusted. Fortunately, plans are underway to etch this into the cornerstones of public buildings.

6. Throughout history, each individual has found the fact of his or her impending demise to be implausible. Most believed they were special. This secret was held closely to their chests. It apparently makes a dry, rattling sound when knocked loose.

7. Punctuation matters: the penis, mightier than the sword?

8. In modern parlance, we have one word for snow. Native peoples, however, had dozens of words for money, including bones, clams, bread, trees, meat, shells, and coca leaves, which, ironically, produce the aforementioned snow.

9. It is not possible to consider the next observation.

10. Directions can be difficult to follow. The authorities are aware of this and have convened a committee to propose solutions. Internal politics are slowing the process, however. As in all things, it is a question of cultivating the proper discipline.

Crow

The crows here
speak the same language

as they do across the sea.
Try to think of another

word for caw.

When I took my
crow to Estonia

he was immediately conversant
and took up

with a polished set
leaving me

alone at the hotel
with the inexpensive

whores, circling.

No matter how long we
sat upon a branch

when the dark cloak
spread and we

leapt into flight—
it felt abrupt.

Nothing to really
crow about—

stitching the ragged
wood together

with flown thread and cawing
that one word

that means everything.

The Date

She took the pink eraser out of her purse and went
to work on his face—not the features so much as the dark
crevasse in his brow and the knowing set of his stony jaw.

Her wrist hinged smooth as oil beneath her hand gliding
like the head of a charmed snake over his cheekbones
softening him so deftly that on a sudden impulse she added

the barest smudge of a dimple, framing his mouth
into something that suggested a coming smile: "What is this?"
he murmured once she'd slipped the pink stub

back into her purse, disguised as lipstick. "What is this I feel?"
The smile of a boy flitted across his face then vanished
as a thunderhead toppled from the summer evening

flushing the asphalt streets with such rain
that if you stood in the rivering gutters, your ankles
would be kissed with cool water while your soles

pressed pavement warmer than blood—that is when

the man walks into the rain with neither umbrella nor overcoat

and you can not tell his crying from the downpour. Inside

she looks into her handheld mirror, drawing her cheeks

taut as she once again wields the slender eraser

and with two swift strokes removes her mouth.

Thought Grenade

Picking the shrapnel of a thought from the softness of an opened
mind once the concussion has stilled into a barely ringing silence
is referred to as *gleaning a slow harvest* in the village of Mataghori.

You may recall that it was Mataghori where over fourteen million
provocative notions were planted in the soil of the river bottom
to slow the massive infantry advance during the last occupation
causing soldiers to pause and ruminate upon what might constitute
a handful of fire or whether migrations of deer in the mountains
can be considered scripture. Rumination means grazing the surface
of the living world and working it down into a paste, and it is true
many soldiers laid down their rifles and began a slow and rhythmic
working of their mental hinges that ended only when pangs of hunger
pierced the reverie and dragged their leather-clad bones toward home.

Now these many years later, the detonations continue, whether struck
by an ox-drawn plow blade or triggered by a child leaping from a tree,
thoughts blossom and leave the stunned victim gleaning a slow harvest,
feeling a hemorrhage of wonderment that not even time can stanch.

from The Book of Time

1. (12:00 a.m.) A great deal hinges upon this point in time, yet in actuality it is not a point but a flutter, a quiet sigh where today's lips gently brush against those of tomorrow. The effects of this can be observed on mourning doves, who visibly shudder at its passage.

2. (2:43 p.m.) Heraclitus once observed that this particular moment was "harder to kill than a rat with a rock." Despite the way it reclines, apparently inert, in the slack hammock of an eternal afternoon, it is composed largely of gristle.

3. (11:14 p.m.) This minute passes with tremendous exactitude, year in, year out, performing its sixty seconds with the piston-like reliability of a Bosnian porn star in spite of our general fatigue and wine-soaked oblivion.

4. (7:42 a.m.) It comes, then goes. Were it a punctuation mark, it would be the dash, as experts have never conclusively determined whether it ultimately wants to separate or connect.

5. (10:59 a.m.) Pope John XXIII once observed 10:59 ante meridian to be his favorite moment of the day, intoning in a papal bull that it is "better to anticipate than arrive" and though eleven o'clock might invoke the perfect ripeness of a plum, "yearning for the honey is totally money."™

6. (6:42 p.m.) This is not a passing moment, but a panther, a feline apparition that is rarely seen, given how deftly its camouflage melts into dappled shadow. It emerges as the sun wheels on its dusky hinge, then stalks us out of curiosity intermingled with appetite.

7. (4:13 a.m.) Here we have the quiet student who fades unremarkably into the background, whom you struggle to recall years later, even after seeing the disturbing headline, the grainy photograph, the feral stare, groping to understand the pain that must have always been there.

8. (1:12 p.m.) Remarkably, no world leader has ever been photographed at this instant, in any time zone. When this was brought to light in a tour de force of investigative journalism at *Le Monde*, in 1974, the paparazzi protested by photographing statues of public figures.

9. (3:33 p.m.) You might recall that this rogue moment was outlawed in Montevideo, Uruguay, in 1888. Riots bloomed like red flowers in the marketplace.

Wind

They decided to inject the wind with dye, so they could follow its circulation. Folding chairs were set up on a hillside, so the group could witness it ravel and unwind. A bin full of clipboards was placed nearby.

Their first observation was that wind crossed open fields in broad sheets. The sheets then frayed, bit by bit, into threads of wind, and then into tiny hairs of wind that were softer than cottonwood down, or milkweed once it has burst from the pod. These shavings seemed content to curl away into nothingness.

The observers leaned forward in their chairs, noting the occasional playful cuff as the wind moved across water, pressing it with a million hands. You could hear a distinct scratching of pencils. One witness was moved to write: "It dipped and lifted away, then dipped again, like a porpoise." The author was pleased enough with this description that she shared it with a colleague, who smiled and nodded.

On the mountain, there was a strong and constant encircling. It was like viewing a rock through the branches of a thicket. It was a licking in the shape of flames, wreathing the rock with snow. Occasionally one gauzy finger pulled away and then collapsed back with a shudder, but this was unusual. Mostly, the wind hugged granite.

This constancy led to raised eyebrows among some of the observers. There was even a coarse double entendre that was only half whispered. We have concluded, however, that these insinuations are more a reflection upon the scientific community, and its impoverished mindset, than any sort of valid commentary upon the current state of wind/rock relations.

The Problem of Measurement

Escaping the collective delusion of precise measurement proved easier than anticipated. Bicycles, candlesticks, coins, bars of soap—they began simply by cutting most things in half, using pruning shears and kitchen knives. Or whatever else was handy.

When absolutists asserted that a theoretical whole still existed—complete and inviolate—they cut everything in half again. Then they cut everything in half again. Once the pattern was established, it was hard to stop.

The benefits were many.

Halving allowed even the uneducated classes to see the prospect of infinity in a glass of milk—which, halved once for every decimal place in π, still held nourishment for a bevy of paramecium. Knowing that postage stamps contained a limitless universe was reassuring for many. People began measuring distances by standing on hilltops and using their hands.

Rulers weren't destroyed but found new uses as garden stakes or fence pickets. Out in the countryside, in the old stone chapels, you could overhear the parishioners whispering to one another: "The essence of God is no more or less divisible than a woolen sock."

She

walked through the door and announced
that the weekend had been mostly fucking

boring. She paused a little, before the *boring*.
This created a tension, which he grasped

like a wire to pull himself upright then
waltzed to the closet where his man suit

hung like skin from a hanger, resembling
nothing so much as an open-mouthed fish.

"Shall I put this on," he inquired in a debonair tone.
"Perhaps we could enjoy an evening of mostly

television." She laughed and unzipped her
feminine wiles, letting them fall around her

legs like a loose curtain. They conceded
they were both hairy underneath, driven

largely by scent. Then it grew suddenly cool.
He checked for drafts. "Nothing can be

done," she murmured. You need more than
storm windows to hold out particular truths.

In the Capital

It is a hillside town: houses stacked
like pottery on shelves. From the window
you see two schoolgirls walking uphill
holding books to their chests, white socks
drooping in the heat. The man painting
the water tank of a building across the valley
has descended to the shade to eat his lunch.
The tank waits impassive as a farm animal,
contemplating the buttery hue of its belly.
Wash is strung on lines like pinioned wings.
The old man on the balcony across from us
is twisting his shirt in heavy ropes to wring
the sunlight from its folds. A small basin
has been positioned below to catch the stream.
What trickles out is cloudier than expected,
a pale yellow liquid the color of young corn,
but it is also faintly luminous and it is this
mundane detail you will remember.

The Differences

Afterward, the most noteworthy change was children
born with polyhedral eyes. This gave many pause.
As always, authorities claimed it was correlative not causal
but the willingness to assume risk was sharply diminished.

With all anomalies there is a desire for elimination.
For instance, the landowner who dispatched a rodent
using the rim of a metal bucket. Don't let the softly angled
voice dissuade you. The speaker himself has killed in this manner.

With children, we know the ancillary symptoms persisted.
The smell of certain cheeses caused distress. Also,
coarse hair grew on finger-backs to the second knuckle.
This became a primary mode of identification: a commonplace

on market days to see women flipping over young hands
like pale crabs, for inspection. *There! What did I tell you?*
Voices triumphant but wrapped in the grimy foil of fear.
Once accommodations were made, such public acts grew rare.

Now it is only the uninitiated, the moronic, and ironically
the hopelessly young who need schooling in the new decorum.
So which of these are you, that you persist with your questions?

The Choice

Pascal might be correct about the agony of human history
resulting from our inability to sit contented in a room alone.

If so, the urge to demolish will strike and when it does
fire is acceptable, and even transfixing, though also strangely

passive when compared to swinging a wrench
in a room full of bones still sheathed and tensing
in the limbs of those dead set on avoidance.

One can sit on a hill, arms clasped about the knees
and watch a barn pulse and roar in seizures of heat.
The smell of gasoline might lift from one cuff as the cinders curl.

Or one can heft oiled steel by the haft and go to swinging work
like a grim berserker in a muddy field, the weight of the axe
straining the ligature, broadening the arc of your reach in the world.

The Buzzard and Reversal

I.

That hooked beak
finds scent and carves
circles above it—

tilting on airy
ridges and shifting
planes and panels, it

leans on one wing,
ascribes the invisible
architecture of rising

air then closes like a door and
falls toward a softness
soon to be opened.

II.

In the dream, there are rabbits. Quiet as ever,
but crowded and jostling round the fallen buzzard.

They ignore the clover where the bird fell, dipping instead
into the dark thatch of feathers with their busy nibblings,
with their tiny snipping teeth. The impossible

softness of their fur is caked with blood. The bird is
broken: a collapsed umbrella. Its naked head emerges
and turns to watch itself drawn shining into the light.

Coming Home

The softness inside the metal shell
smoothed dull by landscape streaming past

is a human family
coming home from northern holiday
    —the children swam

down to the cellar of the pond—
using the moss-furred rope of the raft
    to pull themselves deeper
until chill green water
    brushed their bellies, thrilling them.

    Now,
they slump in the backseat near sleep
burned brown by the sun
loose-limbed as dogs
so they do not know what it is

that will shriek and fling their
bones like straps of weed in a thundering sea.

It will happen soon, in the moment when
they enter the blind spot of the dark sedan
where the driver is considering
changing lanes even now. Quarter panels

will kiss the steering wheel will overcorrect the wheels
beneath will slide like butter in the pan. The air
will slow for the man and woman in the front seat.
They will exchange a glance

that lasts much longer than the moment meant to hold it—
it will seem they have time to contemplate
terror until concrete
arrives to hurtle time
forward on its loosened track—

but for now the man has one
hand on the wheel. The other
lolls on the seatback, flipping his wife's ponytail.
They are singing to the song on the radio. They both
smiled when it first came on, they were so delighted.

Solitude

The notes murmur and stir,
moving like a bag blown across a field, touching
down only between gusts

and if you looked through the doorway and saw the girl on the bench,
you'd probably be surprised that she
is the one drawing such sounds from the piano in the front room,

its endless teeth always waiting
beneath that dark and polished lip.
She lifts the lid and plays while the cat watches,
green eyes narrowing into slits as it approaches

sleep or perhaps bliss—its expression as inconfundible as the music
or the sun falling through the window—
there are dust motes floating in that shaft of light, stirred
by the music in the air

and I know exactly how the cat feels,
lying there in the shaded room as it grows warmer outside,
but I'm not sure you do—

which is a problem, frankly.
You're probably still hung up on inconfundible,
which I'll admit is a poet word if ever I've heard one,
but what if I told you it's precisely

the right word and falls flat
only because you don't happen to speak Spanish?
You're going to insist
that I should have signposted it for you
through the use of italics, as is the convention,

but what if every time I challenge you a bit
I lapse into italics? Wouldn't you feel as if I were talking
down to you, from my incredibly ornate chair on a raised platform,

or, to put it another way, my *throne*.
The fact is, it's too late for italics now—
you've already read the word twice without them,
and if I were to go back to that room,
and the sunlight and the music and the girl

and somehow change it, right behind your very eyes,

that would clearly violate incontrovertible laws

of time and space, revealing powers I'm not ready to share.

Consider for a moment

what would be demanded of me by a hungry populace,

how I would be commandeered,

all the petty concerns that would be laid at my feet:

"Mistakes were made, my youth was misspent, please

unmarry me, allow me to erase

what I spoke in anger, why couldn't she just be

alive for one more day?"

You see the difficulty.

These are not powers to be treated lightly,

and I am unprepared to enter such a realm.

I would need a cape, a suit of invulnerability,

perhaps a fortress of solitude,

and even then I'd still be as lost and alone

as that young girl playing piano, not certain what was moving me,

not even a cat to keep me company.

Rooms and Days

The future is a room with windows and no doors.
The windows are smudged from the noses looking in.

It is a day that is perfect because it never comes.

The ceiling of the room is white as milled paper,
the sunlight of the day an eternal shock to our blinking eyes

as we exit the matinee,
that play of flickering light which engages us so profoundly just now.

That the glass is smudged
is one in many of a long line of examples
of desire obscuring its own object.

That the cinema has been referenced is also apt—
as we compare what is illusory with illusion.

A day and a room: too simple perhaps
to contain life, yet that is what we use them for,

both metaphors barely persisting beneath the stare of the ceiling,
as blank and unyielding as our demands.

Animal

Smelling spring roads after rain
in a car through the luminous green, we

startled a shagginess out from the sycamores.
Horses. Maybe bison. Shadows with hooves?

But no. Just one. One fluid thing. The car
jolted onto the shoulder, spitting gravel,

and then our first soft steps from the asphalt
spilled into the open field. We watched it lunge.

"My god," you said, "That thing's alive."

It circled out to the fence, gathered to leap,
and each buckling movement filled my torso

with terror, with hope, because it was
wild and had torn itself loose from the earth.

The Mind Forest

Words sift through
leaves like deer.
They bed down at dusk
making ovals in the grass.

They sleep a wakeful
sleep shot through
with eddying shivers
ready to spring

so that when we climb
into vehicles and cruise
the reflective ribbons
of rain-soaked freeways

past sodden fields
filled with the ponds
that follow rain—
and suddenly, deer!

bolting lithe through space

doubled above themselves—

we see what might be

said without words.

Man

burrows into his cave
lined with warm earth
dug from the pine hillside.
Roots spiral from above
like coarse hair, fragrant
and beaded with sap.
He digs until he strikes
shattered bedrock buried
like a wisdom tooth
then lights his candle.
How long he carves
signs into the granite
and paints signs onto
the granite, we do not know.
He outlines the trembling
shapes cast by his unsteady
light until at last the flame
draws up straight as thread
and the air around him grows
still and he turns to see

the mouth of the cave

has firmly closed and he

has become a tongue.

II.

At the Café

He was skirting the outdoor tables, smelling faintly of urine,
singing his song and muttering naughty comments that made us

smile, and I wondered how life would have been different
if he'd been my dad. I shared this thought with my companion,

who gave me a look that mingled pity with disgust, which isn't
easy. It seemed it might be wise to keep my musings to myself.

When the salad came, I noted that the sharpness of the dressing
had avoided all hints of bitterness. A miracle of balance, I said.

And I thought I could taste a hint of melon in the wine.
But in reality I was still following the tottering gait of my imagined

father across the plaza, shadowing him through the evening
until he eventually went slack and I carried him back to his den

beneath the overpass, where I wrapped him carefully in his tarp
and waited until his breathing deepened and I knew he was asleep.

The Room

When you die you end up in a room.

Apparently, many people know this. The question, then, is whether this is a waiting room or a destination and why the woman behind the desk is full of smiles. The complimentary coffee is richly brewed and stands beside a small pitcher brimming with cream; the croissants flake away in golden leaves, apparently purchased that very morning. It occurs to you then that it may have been morning for a very long time.

You reach for the reading material, thinking you might find a mailing label to ascertain an address, but the space is blank. The journals hold essays that make you feel better about yourself for having read them. Someone has made certain assumptions about the clientele here and you think this is the sort of place you would like to have your oil changed.

When at a certain point everyone begins to remove their clothes, revealing thick pelts of fur where you anticipated skin, only their pale abdomens remain naked. You feel chagrined knowing what lies beneath your own rumpled clothing. The woman at the desk nonetheless insists that you disrobe, using hand gestures and again that disarming smile.

As you fumble at the buttons it seems your fingers no longer belong to you.

The woman steps out to assist and you immediately understand that she is the caretaker here, so when your clothes fall away at last the pelt beneath is golden brown with lightly dappled camouflage. "You are welcome," she says, gesturing to where daylight has burst through the pocked and crumbling walls and the warm air feels like breath upon your face as you bound across the open fields, amazed.

The Anecdotalist

Remember this one?

Narcissus vs. Pond
in a staring contest?

Wind riffles water,
Narcissus declared winner.

Enraged pond
pulls out hidden revolver.

I don't remember it
ending like that either.

But when the lake
I happened to be dating
re-told the tale at our
holiday cocktail party,

she was a bit tipsy
after maybe six or seven
hundred gallons of vodka.

Normally in the evenings
her moonlit face is serene

as it was on the night
when I first entered her
while skinny-dipping
with my church group.

I felt her touch my stuff
and it clamped against me
snug as a walnut.

When I told my parents,
my father simply stared
unblinkingly at his shoes
while my mother looked
sort of haunted and wistful.

I had heard tell of her
dalliance with a waterfall.

It had ended badly when he
left her, tumbling over granite
in a foaming froth of rage.

"This is different," I insisted.
"This water doesn't run."

Yet here I was now at the party
with a distinctly sinking feeling
and a submerged recollection
of my 7th grade science teacher
tilting a beaker and announcing:

"Water always finds its own level,"

as all the tipsy revelers crowded
more and more closely around her
searching for their reflections
as she gently lapped the shore.

The Taxidermist and The Cloud

The taxidermist looked at the creamy musculature of cumulus

outlined against the blue.
                        "Only the thick stuff from the top,"
he murmured. "And so crisp in this light."

Then he inquired: "How would you like to be this way forever?"

The cloud had yet to hold a pose for even
    the slenderest moment, allowing the slow churn of air to turn
        it always into something

  else.   "I've got rain in the belly and thoughts of roiling
                        up into the body of a thunderhead
before toppling back down in a fine-haired mizzle," said the cloud.

"But I could capture you from the best angle
                        and make you beautiful
forever," said the taxidermist.
              "And how long would that be?" asked the cloud.

"Longer than you can remember in both directions,"

                                   said the taxidermist.

The cloud sighed. "I can only always remember myself

         as water through and in the above and the drenching

deep into the soil until bearded roots pull me through green

                                   bodies into sky.

                I am both verb and ocean."

"That's not a bad little speech,"

                said the taxidermist, lighting a cigarette.

He inhaled the smoke hungrily through his nose like a wolf

                           and sent a miniature

cloud from his throat. "Very funny,"

said the cloud.   A strange odor hovered in the air, like singed tin,

                          before the crackling bolt struck.

In The Land of My Fathers

Should someone ask if you would like a draught
of blood-black rioja to melt like chocolate in the warm

pan of your mouth, the traditional response is not
a simple, "Yes, please," but rather the imperative,

"Pleasure me." Your blade hovers above choice meat as you pause,
the words invariably accompanied by a brief moment

of eye contact. Waiters who deliver heart-felt smolder
in this momentary flutter command the wages of starlets

and rainmakers. The mutual shift to indifference that occurs
mere seconds later does little to discourage

an after-scent of cumin and lavender from lingering
in the air. Would you like some bread? Pleasure me.

And do you wish the butter to be warmed in the secret
corners of my body? Pleasure me. Would you like to be touched,

here, in elfin whispers? Pleasure me. All this must be communicated
by sensitive eyes, so should you wander the gravel paths of a park

on a Sunday, you will see them there, reclining in the sun
on green wooden benches, dozens of waiters, gazing at the clouds,

                                        eyes hidden behind dark glasses.

The Doppelgängster

sat opposite me on the train,
                        hands folded loosely in his lap,
fingers tangled like copulating starfish,
                                his gaze level
with my own in a sort of deadpan monotone. We both wore
a bit of stubble.
                  I've gone silver in the muzzle; his whiskers
too were tipped with frost.
              His pale skin was underscored
with blue while mine was sun-warmed brown.
                                "I see you," he said.
Then: "I see you too,"
          he said again.
              "Is this the beginning of a novel?"
I thought to ask but didn't.
                Instead I reached inside my jacket
and withdrew a heavy silver pen received as a gift.
                                  I carry it
mostly for its pleasant heft. When I looked up I saw that he
had unfolded the blade of a hunting knife.

"The pen holds the tale by the end. Or so I've heard."

"The tail of the tiger," he averred. "At the end of the day, sword is just another word."

There Is Nothing

There is nothing
        better than feeling the cold
                soft earth of spring

  against soles grown thin
and tender from months of dozing inside
wool and boots
    released to feel the fine prick of winter grass
and the frost
    still asleep beneath the sun-warmed earth

We walk slowly
              And when the animal rises
from the hill not far away

            it is as if the land has given
birth to its own scrawny hunger

                        It watches us

with wary eyes and we go

                silent

    in an attempt to speak a few words

in the ancient common tongue

                        Its moist nose flares

to drink them in and what I fear

            is that I might recollect this

in a way that makes it larger

                    or more fearsome

than what it simply is: a river

living inside a skin that has grown claws

                to open things   Like me

The Weight of a Shadow

There is *nothing* to say
and I am most certainly the one to say it

as my life's work
has been crafting a silence
to fit the exact shape of what it was
that needed saying

Now I'm ready
to put my arms around someone
shaped more or less like me

whose strange heart
will beat against my sternum
as we embrace and disappear

leaving the place in the air
where our bodies were

to close behind us
without a scar—

The Ottoman

I did not anticipate when the ottoman moved
that it would hump along like a sea lion. Normally
one does not begin anecdotes about moving furniture
with furniture that moves of its own volition. But
that's what happened. The overstuffed ottoman
arched its upholstered back and lunged out the door
the minute it opened, scuttling madly for the sea.
I did not understand its need for haste. I simply
stood in the doorway and watched it awkwardly
drag itself across the beach, furrowing the sand.
Then I turned to see the long-necked polar bear
emerge from the darkened hallway behind me. "Ahh,"
I said, "this now makes perfect sense." And I quietly
lay down so that the bear might begin to dine.

The Woman

She sat with her hands in her lap for nearly twenty years
then smiled and wandered to where they'd piled up the poems.

Using a ballpoint pen, she began to subtitle each and every one.

This would have been a rather complex undertaking
had she not discovered that most of the time only three words
were necessary: *Look at me. Look at me. Look at me.*

Her observation was not merely cheeky; it became genuinely
visionary when she penned the *me* using transparent ink
so that readers might look through and beyond the rain-
spotted pane into shadowy hallways they had yet to wander.

The Delicate Skull of a Small Animal

Where are you?   Hiding behind the darkened trees.

Which tree?   Only those that were fed by rain.

Are you everywhere?   (Chuckles.) No.

Then how can that be?   There are so many of me I have lost count. I have even spent some time as you.

I don't believe you.   Of course not. I did not believe me either. Now reach into your pocket and see what I left there for you, gleaming like snow and clean

                                        as the wind—

Stephen

plinked out melodies on the piano
right hand stepping among the keys
naked animal nosing down an alleyway
sniffing idly for the right note
or the merely plausible one—

once it rang out the chain complete
that bare-knuckled spider would
retrace its steps three maybe four
times mechanically no thought
to musicality as if pressing a code
into a keypad because Stephen
believed memory was housed
in the meat and cord of the body.

He peeled aromatic clementines
into tenuous spirals and quietly
cursed when the damp skin broke.

He took the dog on long walks
and left her leashed outside bars,
friendly tail sweeping the pavement
at the approach of every stranger
while he hunched philosophically
over his foam-stained glass inside.

Habits are the pattern in the weave
and you've now been offered three
framed straight as I could manage.

If there is another way to keep
Stephen here among us now,
in this world of fruit, dogs and
breathing lies, I do not know it.

Humbleman

1

He aspired to imitate Jesus
as a model of humility. This
proved to be complicated.

But he persevered,
acquiring the pseudonym
Humbleman the Lesser,

and he captained the nation
in the humility Olympics
in Gståad in 1934,

where the podium was
a ditch and the winner
descended the stairs

until he disappeared.

2

You may recall
he won five events

and was so riven
with hot-faced shame

he held his medals
defiantly aloft

until nervous officials
declared them rescinded,

permanently uncarving
his anonymous fame

from a mountain face
that does not exist.

Hedgehog

The man and the woman had a house with beautiful pictures on the walls. They shopped from catalogs. They took care of their bodies by walking up treadmill staircases. They were intelligent enough to see the metaphoric possibilities of this endeavor, but steady enough not to go there. They had sexual intercourse once a week. They had no children.

But when the man went to the bar a few blocks from his house, his neighbors made lewd insinuations. "How is it that one who owns so much cannot manage to accomplish what dogs can?" they wondered aloud. "Does someone need instructive videos on intercoursing a female?"

The man smiled tightly and continued to watch the hockey game. It was easy enough to tune them out. If he blurred his eyes, the skaters looked like water striders. The goalie lurched like a primate, bobbing his head in its oversized mask. But as the man walked home three beers later, he lost his temper and swore and said, "I will have a child even if it's a hedgehog."

So when the child was born, of course, it was a hedgehog. This would have been really painful had it not come out headfirst, but as it happened, the birth went with the grain of the boy's quills and was quite easy, given his tapered snout and the girth of his ribcage.

The boy seemed a bit lost in the bedroom they'd decorated for him, but was happy enough once he discovered the terrarium stocked with dried figs, crickets, and mealworms. His father had bought him a pair of suede skateboard shoes, knowing full well that it might take a while to grow into them. "Who knows what he'll gravitate toward," he shrugged. "I just thought they looked well-made."

Yet the boy was fond of them. His parents filled them with cedar shavings and he burrowed into them at bedtime, alternating between the left and right. They often crept into his room late at night and watched him sleep, his pink legs twitching as he dreamed of chasing moths.

The One-Time Monster

The monster did not care about clichés when he contacted me
from under the bed. "I am here," he said, using a voice in my mind,
"and I will in all likelihood destroy you, with teeth like ivory knives."

"These teeth do not fit properly inside my mouth. They peek
out like tusks from my dark lips. But I am not hungry right now,"
he said, and he lay there, quietly, waiting to see what I would do.
"So much hair," I said. It was thick between my fingers and my hands
disappeared into his pelt. "That feels good," he said. "No one has ever

touched me that way." "No one?" I asked. "No, they are too afraid
of these teeth leaving puncture wounds in their gut and how
I might shred long strips of muscle from their bones." "Oh," I said.
"Plus, you are the first person I ever met," he said, "because I am
a one-time monster." "What is that?" I asked, even though I already
knew. He just looked at me, his brown eyes patient like a dog.
I thought about freezing with terror, but he was too smart for that.
"Thanks," he said after a while, "but would you please just let me go?"

The Important Book

The book said, "There is another world inside of this one,"
so we started peeling everything carefully away.

I began with the leather chair, revealing just how much
air there is in furniture. Hardwood frame, metal coils,
shreds of remnant wool. "Architecture is mostly boxes
of air," I thought, and then I wondered what is inside
air but epic space between the molecules: that is when
we stopped singing and everyone looked into the bonfire.

It seemed the book was right: there is
another world inside of this one and it might well be
empty. The wine bottle passed from hand to hand
as we pulled lathework free to feed the flames.
No one heeded when I later slipped the book
into my bag and caught the last train home.

I hurried up the steps and let the book
fall open on the kitchen table
where it immediately projected a steady incandescent
beam upon the ceiling. "How quaint," I thought,
as I contemplated the semi-bright glow, a little
disappointed by the cliché, not really caring
where the illumination came from. I lifted a hand

to turn the page when I saw the crisp outline
of a seabird—a gannet, to be specific—
silhouetted against the ceiling. Its wings
were scissored back, its body a white arrow

poised to fall into the green water and silver
fish crowding the shallows. Then I took
my other hand and placed it above the stream
to watch a cockroach shimmy in the blankness.
My head was an opened flower, my cock
a crescent wrench. My entire body curled
into a ball and balanced deftly on the book
proved to be nothing more than a singed leaf.

Change
after Pu Songling

He was gaunt, his skin like a wet windbreaker stretched across chain-link. He begged downtown, sitting on a woven mat, muttering a prayer for each coin that clinked into his coffee can.

He refused all paper money—and any other offerings—and was never seen to eat or drink. He fished the shiniest coins from the can, mostly pennies, and set them in neat rows along the edge of his mat, creating an outline of his station, sometimes leaving them behind when he rolled up his mat and disappeared.

"Spare change," he said, quietly and repeatedly. "Spare change."

His inflection did not rise at the end. There was no hint of deference. I often reflected as I passed him that he offered the words as a quiet imperative.

"Why don't you leave here?" I asked him one day. "Away from the diesel and the smell of gasoline." I looked at the soot darkening the creases of his body. "You can pray just as well in the park, or among the pines at the edge of town."

"That," he said simply, "is not the change that I am seeking."

I was there when the authorities finally confronted him. New laws had gone into effect. The patrol was kind but firm: he would have to move along.

At first he seemed dazed. But as he began to understand that he was being told to leave, he grew agitated, then furious. He produced a penknife from the folds of his filthy jacket, opened it with a click, and drew it sharply and deeply across his belly with a ragged sound.

For a moment, I half expected a waterfall of coins to come surging out. Instead he began pulling out the shining ropes of his viscera, madly, like a man emptying snakes from a basket. The patrol radioed for help. He was dead within minutes.

The horrified officials gave his corpse a hasty burial in a field at the edge of town. It was a place crisscrossed by paths, with shredded plastic bags caught in the briars, shivering like jellyfish.

When a dog dug into the grave a few days later, the edge of his woven mat could be seen, wrapping the bulge of his body. I came close and touched it gently with my boot and felt a hollowness. When I returned with a spade to examine it more closely, I found it empty as the husk a cicada leaves behind.

When He Lay Down Beneath the Earth

We didn't know what to do when he lay down
beneath the earth and began dreaming grass
in shades of green we'd never seen before.
"Are you dead?" we asked. "Not exactly," he said.

A flower came from his mind and bloomed,
its petals unfolding like crinkled wings in the sun,
just as they would in a time-lapse film of a moth
emerging from chrysalis, and we said, "Nice work."

He just nodded. Or I should say tried to nod,
given how firmly he was rooted into the dark soil.
His tangled hair and beard had become a nest
for the eggs of his features: nose, cheekbone, brow.

When a bee hummed into the blossom and waded
through its stamens, he didn't flinch. That's when
we knew beauty spawns honey and venom both
and we quit holding our tongues and began to sing.

III.

Afterward

One hundred and twelve years from now, the scattered tribes
made their way north. They skirted the hulks of eaten cities,
the weed-shattered pavements long since turned to gullies.

Stories came down from the poles: instructions and diagrams
said to be there, things considered essential human knowledge,
belief in an island beyond Norway housing archives of crop seed.

They'd heard repetitions of syllables: *appetite*, *equilibrium*, and again
and again a musical term: *harmony*, as a sort of warning. The stories
circled back on themselves, ending always with the same words:

Time itself will end, but you cannot ask what that means.

Cities were rust and danger. Little looked as it once did.
It grew warm. Kudzu came north. Nothing evolved to eat it.
Ruins were covered in fibrous vines, speared with ailanthus. Cellars

filled with algae bloom, then silted in. The land swarmed green,
but barren. Hungry cattle near the coast waded into marshland,
and sharks, grown large and abundant, swam upriver to feed,

the water thick with muscle. Coral crept northward too,
leaving ghosted reefs in warm water, showing bone-white
through mats of slime. Re-acquaintance with rain, heat and

vigilance changed the remaining clans. Language grew simpler.
Even with scavenged books and the desperate teaching the confounded,
words were lost. On hillsides, camps flickered with the sooty flame

of rags stuffed into cans. Then darkness. Things scavenged, not made.
The rarity of children. It was understood that what was buried, persists.

The Operation

The children stood in line outside the office, pressing their small bodies into doorways when the rain began. More a mist than a rain, really. It was the soft whiteness of a low cloud.

At regular intervals—every four minutes, say—the blue door opened and another child was admitted. For a flickering moment a face would lift in silhouette toward an unseen voice, then two damp shoes would busily wipe themselves on the mat. It must have been a part of the routine, reminding them.

With a touch on the shoulder, the assistant guided them down the hallway and into a room with two slatted wooden chairs. "Have a seat," she said, indicating a point midway between the two.

If they chose the correct chair, the doctor came in, with his gold-rimmed spectacles and a smile deepening the lines around his eyes. If they chose the wrong chair, the operation was performed. This was monitored through the two-way mirror.

Once the imagination was removed, it was placed on a tray using a pair of ivory-handled tongs. Stripped of its fancy, it was no bigger than a seed.

If it is placed between the back molars and cracked open, it is astonishingly bitter—the bitterness of almond husks, used in the tanning of leather. The taste lingers. Visions supposedly occur.

The Nineteenth Century

She lived simply, with a maid who answered my call peering from behind the heavy door like a schoolgirl. Before I could be announced, her mistress had appeared behind her like a gauzy shadow. I was struck at how quietly she moved, nary a rustle of silk.

"You came," she said, smiling politely.

The careful mask of her face gave away little. Yet I sensed a minor chord. Not surprise, exactly. Rather, there was something in her manner that might be called sly—if I may use so untoward a word.

"I wrote, and you came," she repeated, and suddenly seemed quite pleased. "Come upstairs. You mustn't think it vulgar, but I've been bathing in the morning light, in the sun parlor. It overlooks the garden."

The grounds were laid out in the French style. I found the neat geometry of lavender soothing as she spoke of her husband's business in the city and of our evening with Lady Semadór. The cypress hedge threw long shadows across the grass, their outlines ghosted with dew. With a start I realized that the day was not yet advanced. In my eagerness, I'd called at an absurdly early hour.

"But this is dreadful," I said aloud, interrupting her.

"Indeed," she murmured. "I daresay there's more to life than all this chatter. We must enter the day—"

"But I fear—"

"Nonsense," she smiled, lifting one delicate white hand toward me. "Come. We'll stroll the gardens. The peonies have not yet shed their petals."

The peonies were indeed lovely, their dense heads burst open in striated riots of wine and cream. It was there that I first saw them, near the base of the green stalks. I initially took them for statuary, but the curl of the toes and the grayish tinge on the soles suggested otherwise. They looked as if they had seen recent use.

When she saw where my gaze had come to rest, her dark eyes flashed.

"Ah," she laughed gaily. "I see you've found my feet."

"I must beg pardon, my lady, but—"

She smiled patiently, and modestly lifted the hem of her skirt to confirm the fact. I looked down to see that she was floating, a few inches above the gravel path. Her legs simply ended.

Once I'd recovered myself, I made to gather her feet from where they lay beneath the flowers, but her voice grew quickly cool. "Please, leave them alone. This is all my husband's doing; he will no doubt fetch them once he's home from the city."

Later, when we had tea in the conservatory, her legs were folded beneath her on the wicker divan, and I saw the end of one peeking from beneath the folds of her gown. It looked as if it had been sawn clean, like the chilled cuts of pork at the butcher. It looked like pink glass.

Unhinged

The girl left her house and went into the woods.
The ground seemed to swallow the sound of her

footsteps, and yesterday's rain lifted the smell
of leaves into the pink cushions of her lungs.
Her nostrils flared to drink the loamy scent.
She wore a blue wool coat with a blue wool belt.
Her gaze wandered over the thinning understory,
not fully seeing it, her mind walking different paths
in different tangled places. She had two coins,
one tucked into each pocket so they would not
clink and give her away. Her fingers worked them,
knowing a vanilla steamer awaited her at some
undisclosed point in the future but for now
the anticipation was even sweeter than the yen.

When she left these woods and wandered home,
these coins would no longer possess their value.
Their inability to purchase anything would be
the least of her concerns once she ascertained
the distance she had travelled, but she would
nonetheless remember the sting of the affront
when the young man at the coffee shop pushed
both coins brusquely back across the counter,
his glance communicating he was not inclined
to put up with acts of blatant foolishness.

She would soon learn the coins were tokens
of a past many wished forgotten, but also
that they served as useful evidence of the journey
she had somehow undertaken. Her little brother,
who had been gnawing cold melon rind to relieve
the pain of teething on the day that she had left,
was a married man when next she saw him,
and smelled disturbingly like her father
when he proffered an awkward hug at the reunion
where his daughters made a point of being kind.

On the evening she returned from the woods,
breathless to tell her mother about the cheek
of the boy at the coffee shop, she found another
family inside the house. The new mother answered
the door and held her hand to her mouth while
the girl cried and repeated her last name and the
new mother looked beyond the girl to the woods
while the girl looked beyond the new mother
to different furniture in different arrangements,
both sets of eyes worried, disbelieving, desperate
as a cold understanding began to dawn that neither
girl nor mother would ever be fully at home again.

Things No One Expected to Be True Until Viewing the Film

The imaginary cities of my youth
actually exist.

It turns out a handful
were painstakingly crafted in miniature
by a loose collection of savants in the attics of Vienna,

the rest are nestled in the valleys
that crinkle the foothills of the Carpathians.
Each contains a building on its outskirts

housing an identical wooden spindle chair
painted an inexplicable shade of red.

In some circles, this would be considered
a type of necklace.
An atlas containing photogravure

maps and detailed city plans
also exists

though it has been mislaid
in a bookstore in Buenos Aires,
erroneously filed under

fiction where it has since been
swallowed by contemporary mystery.
Given that a cat's tongue

is the cleanest thing in nature
for centuries the women of the Gøeshtl hinterland
have used that sandpapery pink

for ritual cleansing and exfoliation.

When it comes to the subject of human
geography my peninsula extends
precariously into the cold

waters of the North Sea.
The bay that constitutes
your psyche is shallow and considerably

more storm-tossed than surrounding waters. Also,
your imaginary cities do not exist.
We waited until the credits rolled to confirm this.

But these cities do not exist.
We seem to have reached an impasse
here, an impregnable space

between the reader and her intended
progress—but in all likelihood
it is not due to the tiny

avalanche that recently cascaded
down those papier-mâché mountains
in a Viennese garret. No,

that was simply a handful of loose gravel
and will be swept clean by whisk broom and dustpan.

Orpheus and Eurydice

There they are: walking single file through caverns vast as sky.

It's one of those stories that cannot end: wan light leaks down from above.
They are close enough now that a few sickly flowers grow in the
    cracked rock.

Her slender arms glide through the gloom—pale eels in a murky pool
                                      and once again he turns

                  to look

and sees her drawn back into the pit
            sudden as a scrap of cinder inhaled by a chimney.

In this moment he feels something enter his chest.
    It splits its husk and plants itself in the soil of his body,
sending out white roots to weave a tissue around his heart. They are fine
    as hair
                          and draw upon both warmth and pulse
                                          to feed his song.

Her Wrath

The only thing
I can compare it to
is a pallet of bricks

suspended above me
and the rope snapping.
Actually,

after reflection,
to be completely honest,
there are other things.

There are also nails,
driven into my hands,
pushing aside

the small bones,
and rusted wire
against my gums

would also be good.

It would be apt.

Then we could examine

the similes,

in which her wrath is like

an iron hook in my heart,

like gravel sifting

into my inner ear,

or like a potato

being slowly peeled

and then the peeler

going to work

on me—

my knuckles to be exact.

Her wrath can definitely

be just like that.
Which also recalls
the time her wrath

was like a flower
that never fully opened,
the tips of the petals

turned a papery brown
and the blossom bowed
heavily

in silent prayer.
It was almost as if
I'd seen her

wrath transformed
into something like
sadness or even

patience and it was
then I understood
that this endlessly

inventive anger
was something
I'd written upon her

again and again
like the punishment
of a schoolboy

or the opening lines
of a letter you
write but never send.

Parable

Maybe it's like this: you
walk down a hill at dusk and see

a dark sack at wood's edge
packed heavy and settled

so dark it looks damp—
acorns, grain, sand, stone?

You wonder at the forgetful collector
who left it behind when

it lifts startled into the tossing
green boughs and you understand

it was a bear, solid and quickly
gone: isn't it true
you have looked for years

at some words and also
thought they were heavy?

Report from Beyond
after Herbert

In paradise the work week is fixed at thirty hours
and manual labor is only pleasantly more tiring than typing
so that a morning chopping wood is barely enough
to make the ham sandwich and the cold bottle of beer
a bit more delicious at the rough wooden table afterward

Punctuation is underused because words flow one into
the other like branching streams of snowmelt wrinkling
over rough granite into alpine meadows where tiny stars
pass themselves off as flowers and the children weave
green stems into crowns which are the only trappings worn
by the rulers who are wise and listen intently to their subjects
without merely thinking of what words they will offer in response

The parks are clean the social system stable and the new
eight-day week has created a gentle hammock of time
in what used to be Sunday evening where the bells toll
and streets are closed so families might stroll the avenues

Old men still wear their pants too high public fountains
are still fish-scaled with coins the authorities have yet to
solve how the smell of frying food hangs in the air for hours

At first the great beyond was to have been quite different
each life was to have comprised one note in the harmonious
thrum of a cosmic chord but they found it too difficult
to reduce even simple lives to a single sound and a gluey
paste kept getting caught at the back of the angels' throats

God has yet to make an appearance but this absence is
common fodder for the rumors which suggest he wanders
among them as a breeze so they see not him but his evidence

The Invisible Book

Sometimes when I'm reading,
I'm distracted by the invisible
book underneath the book
I'm actually reading and the problem

is this: it's better. It's like
the superball under the couch
that your fingertips barely brush:
the slightest contact and it's

gone, gliding easily away,
because its form is nearly
perfect, there, a sphere
in the darkness and dust.

You can't get to this book
so you read the other one,
the actual fabric and paper
tilting in your hand, whose
primary virtue is suggesting
the other, hinting at the unseen

that was whispering something
wonderful into existence
as the pen wrote down slightly
different words, approximations,
compromises, all those choices
that seemed good enough,
maybe even thrilling, at the time.

The Dinner Party

We realized later that no one had been paying
attention to how much he had been drinking
so there was disbelief and oddly pitched laughter

when he stood on the coffee table one shoe
resolutely mashing a soft cheese we had all
favorably commented upon while he smiled

and kept trying to lift his t-shirt to show us the
alterations his wife grasping at him saying lets
not do that right now while he slapped her

away as if it were some kind of private tickling
game that had gone a little too far then clutched
her wrists suddenly sober and said they need

to see while she shook her head no but stepped
back and stopped fighting him as he lifted his shirt
and unzipped himself from navel to sternum

with a sound that was surprisingly wet then

opened himself so we could hear the voices

rise in a harmonic chorale that shook the house.

Other People

The day was too bright at the abandoned café
scoured clean by April wind as you held my hand

almost lovingly and said, "Maybe we should start
seeing other people," and suddenly there they were,

absentminded in their mismatched clothes, all around us,
the people we had been unable to see until that point

because we had been so involved in seeing one another.
But then your words conjured them from the very air,

these other people we so clearly needed to begin seeing
if we didn't want to keep fooling ourselves, which was

another phrase you used, and I suddenly understood
why I sometimes felt oddly wooden, like a poorly hinged

door when I leaned in to kiss you—it had to be that
elderly woman with the permanently puckered mouth

and cardigan laced with cat hair who stood like a shadow
behind your right shoulder, fiercely glaring and happy

to finally be making eye contact with me after so many
futile attempts to serve as your matronly avenger.

Why she was holding an enormous scythe I cannot say,
any more than I could pronounce the surname of the

Estonian mechanic who stood so patiently beside her,
hefting a lightly oiled wrench in one grimy hand.

I rose in what I hoped was a dignified manner and strode
out through the gathering crowd, shaking hands with

the blacksmith sporting mutton chops and a svelte man
in suede boots and a remarkably slimming goatskin vest,

when it occurred to me that the fluttery pain near my heart
was not sadness but relief at no longer being so utterly alone.

The Shadow

It was five o'clock. He left the room and returned by six, having grown a full beard. It looked velvety in the dusky light. On some level everybody wished to touch it, just as we are drawn to the impossible softness of rabbit fur.

This was all the more striking, as he was twelve and holding a rooster. A woman approached and said,

"Nice cock."

None of this happened, of course. This vignette exists only in the mind's root cellar. The boy never left the room. The woman remained in Berlin, applying mascara.

They sat in their separate locales for the duration, clean-shaven and contemplative. Observers concluded we should be grateful our thoughts don't cast shadows.

The Goat

The goat does not shy from the blade but edges
forward to smell the last goat the knife opened:
its soft nostrils tremble to milk scent from the
metal with a tentative hunger that troubles me:

bristling rope wraps the back legs tight as a vine
then the pitch of its bleating shifts as the slack is
tossed over a low branch and it is winched upside
down above the knife-scarred metal basin strewn
with glossy thumbs of peeled garlic and quartered
onions—it hangs silent now: a pendulum that turns

heavily, threaded with blood, the blade that relaxes
the neck is unexpectedly small, the man who does it
unexpectedly murmuring into one twitching ear
as the pan begins to fill and the golden eyes go slack.

The Limb

The question wasn't whether to tell them about his extra limb, but how.

Words failed him, of course. He'd never told anyone beyond his Aunt Ursula.

Her only accommodation had been to acknowledge it in her knitting. The result was the limb stayed warm in winter, but remained unmentioned in blended company. This arrangement might not have garnered approval from child psychologists, but it developed in William a keen sense of the unspoken.

Surprisingly, scouting trips hadn't been a problem. But as he neared manhood, he naturally wished to mix with others. Autumn found him in a clearing in the sunstruck woods. Yellow leaves fluttered in the light as William tried out possible openings,

"Have you ever wondered how—"

"Don't tell me you've never seen—"

"What would you say if I told you—"

When a cloud crossed the face of the sun and it grew suddenly cold, he unknotted his limb-sweater and took it out.

He stood still for a moment. Then he rocked his body over its unusual fulcrum and started across the clearing. The motion was surprisingly fluid. He moved like a bent wheel, hurling himself forward until he was spinning among the trees with astonishing power.

History

Dusk. Mountains dark against sky, land falling abruptly
into water. Light fading, but still pale above the gone sun.
Vast water beneath stray clouds. They are thin, not much more

than smoke, and higher in the dome, deep blue pierced
with early stars. Everything is softened, washed in lilac grey.
The planes drone out of the north, fat bellied. They hold their line

steadily and look heavy in the air. If you've seen a full-bodied fly
endlessly circling, a beetle whirring over an evening meadow,
you know the sense of weight, the sense of momentum. They cross

the darkening water. The first climbs, banks steeply, then climbs
again. The second follows suit. Their black silhouettes move
like a single animal, bones hinging in a single spine. And then

the poetry of bodies falling from airplanes. Like cinders.
Like black petals. On board, there is pandemonium:
soldiers roped into cargo bays, bayonets fixed, the doors

easing open, the wild suck of wind and hair whipping faces.

The first victims careen out, uncomprehending. Then

the scramble as others grip whatever is at hand and soldiers prod

until bodies slice and wheel into the night. They trail steadily

from the planes, limp bits of rag and silent from this distance;

the only sound is the droning engines. It is a steady thrum. And then

the first plane levels off, empty, and then the second,

and then they all level off, empty, and carve a new line toward home.

Wrecked

We were driving a small station wagon that has now spent
six winters of quiet rust in a midwestern salvage yard
bending the sky above its curved windshield without cease.
Colonies of insects have lived and died in its weed-twined hulk.

The crash itself sounded like a brown paper bag blown fat
then popped loud as a gunshot in a tiled gymnasium; the car
struck the concrete divider, the hood buckled, glass rained
sharp pebbles across my nose split clean open, and my hands
flung up like startled birds. Now, sifting from the piney
scruff edging the junkyard, silent as whitetails, we come:

my son toddling with his broken collarbone my wife wincing
under her cracked ribs the terrorized gaze of our daughter
floating in the dusk and my shirt heavy with its dark stain. Though
years have passed, we are not ghosts. The word is too simple
for what we have become out here in the woods in our hovel
of bark and bent branches with no need for a campfire to warm us.

Excavation

Finally, one came from the rubble whole
and heavy as we rubbed a dull shine into it:
a fired clay vessel. The cracked tallow seal
slipped from the jar easy as a coin, beneath it,
another seal, or so we thought, until somebody
picked with a chisel tip and sniffed the broken
grains then tasted and said the word aloud: "honey."

We smiled in a sort of wondering disbelief
and crowded round to sample crumbs of that
ancient sweetness and speak of what blossoms
might have been worked in this valley by bees
eight hundred years ago. We called it a golden
trove—the jar was deep as my arm to the elbow.
Within a week we made another discovery:

the infant folded inside, the honey a preservative,
the vessel serving as tomb for the stillborn child.
We watched the fine cursive of its bones laid
out carefully against the green felt, blinking white
under the noon sun, born dead a second time.
Nobody would speak of what we first shared,
the nibble we thought we'd stolen from time.

Chain Store

We walked into the store and asked for the elastic notebook. The clerk looked at us, affecting a sort of blank nonchalance. But the signals were there: the rising scent of cumin, the dilation of pupils, and a fluttering of the tiny blood vessels in her neck.

She turned brusquely, slipped behind the counter, and began climbing the ladder.

"I don't think so," said Martin, seizing the cuff of her slacks.

He held firm but didn't tug. No one wanted to see her fall. She was not a young woman.

The ladder was made of slowly turning fire, which caused it to give a little. She clung to the rungs with tenacity. Let's take a moment to imagine what it did to her hands, hanging there.

The Sentence

Life is uttered. A momentary sentence.
There is no white light. Once it has passed,

something else breathes in its stead, a knowing joke
among huddled acquaintances. An intern arrives
to scatter a handful of cloud. No one has seen her before.

Words that once sounded good fall like wet leaves,
adhering to virtually everything then gone by spring.

When you leave, no one checks your pockets.
No one wonders whether your cupboards are clean.
No one finds the knife in your boot, silent as a bone.

Odds

I've been alive for sixteen thousand and ninety days
which means that in sixteen thousand and eighty-nine
of those days I have not been in an accident where I
felt the car fishtail into a glide looked at my wife uttered
"fuck" in the most feeling sense of that ancient syllable
felt our little wagon slam nose-first into concrete
hood flailing back like a broken wing catastrophic noise air
bag snapping my head back cleanly splitting my nose while
we spun in holiday traffic and honking cars wove around us
like a hurtling school of tuna until we crept to a stop and I
stood outside the crumpled rear door jerking a broken
handle the screaming face of my son registering no sound.

On sixteen thousand and eighty-nine of those days I did
not sit unplanned broken stunned on the rainy shoulder
of a Minnesota road gravel smelling of iron not feeling
anything words knocked clear into perfect blankness.

On sixteen thousand and eighty-nine of those days I didn't lose my virginity in anxious sweat break my neck put my dog down feel the jolt of earth come up through my bended knee see my daughter come wide-eyed into the world see my son come bull-shouldered I didn't search for a pulse in the small bones of my grandfather's wrist and call my mother to say I'd held his hand as he'd died. On sixteen thousand and eighty-nine of those days I did not make the decision to sit here and write this all down nor did the decision make me. It didn't happen. Then it did and not because of some line etched across my nose or the fused ribs inside my wife or the surprisingly large feathered cask of the bald eagle's body perched in the oak this morning when I walked with my son and he pointed up and exclaimed and I could hear every word.

Breathless

Today I rose and put on summer
clothes and sat in the corner chair.
I can't say when I first settled
into the habit of noticing wind
in the trees. I do it and wonder
about how things began. Wind
and leaf-shimmer: the all of it.

If you read the first book, it was
finished at chapter one: in the image
he created them, male and female
he created them. But then this
out of clay, that from the other:
the lack of childhood memory,
rapt in dark bone and suddenly

woman, stunned in the new
light, the necessary thrum of bees
pulsing everywhere and nowhere—
she closed her eyes to shut it out.
He didn't know good, evil, her name.
It was orchard and garden all around.
They must have found themselves

locked into a position that left them
breathless. Because there was a first time—
even and especially without words
to ask or raise the possibility of asking
like *even* and *especially* or *how was it*
because there was nothing but garden
all around and no shadow of leaf-litter
beneath the outline of even a single tree.

Hair

When we make a wish for the death of a person we hate,
it has been customary for us since olden times to take a handful of our own hair
to the small shrine at the edge of the village and pray.
—KASUYA EIICHI, "Record of a Strange Tale"

It is true such a wish should only be made once in a lifetime.
It is also true, as Eiichi informs us, that anyone can go to this place
in the dead of night across a bridge made of slowly turning fire.

But what is most true is that the shrine is not a shrine at all.
It is just a place among the trees where an enormous amount
of human hair is scattered among the pine duff and rough bark.

You know you are in the right place when the fine hairs
on your own neck bristle and you see a tree looking
for all the world as if it has begun to dream itself into an animal.

This is when you begin to pray, though with what words,
Eiichi does not say. Instead he paints a portrait of silence and treetops
tasseled with tufts of hate, which has become more than a lifelike thing.

Should you choose to leave a lock of your own here, it will sober you. Perhaps it is better to wheel around and return home, so the clippings on the barber's floor or an unraveling piece of twine will not haunt you.

June

Stray hair is pulled from the lapel of her favorite
wool coat years later in a secondhand shop, drawn
free in a quick, definitive gesture that could only
be called thoughtless. It settles on the worn carpet
while another woman's hand holds the hanger and
drapes the coat across her chest—she eyes it

in the mirror with an air of cold appraisal, breath
rising and falling, her chest plumbed with valves
pulsing mindlessly, the forgotten hair underfoot
still holding the map and code of everything
another woman was: the face with the furrowed brow
that could fold and break into a lightning smile,
a woman with a knack for contentment and
quick anger that dispersed as clouds over hills.

An arm slips in and she feels the cool silk lining
on her bare skin. It is June. She does not need a coat
but her mind craves autumn and being wrapped
in well-wrought layers. She slips the other arm in
and hugs herself, snugging the coat to her waist,

wrapping it like a kimono, "Yes," she thinks, seeing an older version of herself walking through a park—
the image comes suddenly, like rain from nowhere.

Acknowledgments

Grateful acknowledgements are due to the editors of the following publications where many of these poems first appeared: *10x3, The 22 Magazine, 32 Poems, Asymptote, Bateau, Beloit Poetry Journal, Berkeley Poetry Review, Blackbird, Blueline, BOAAT, Booth, Boxcar Poetry Review, Carolina Quarterly, Chicago Quarterly Review, The Collagist, Copper Nickel, Flyway, Forklift Ohio, Four Way Review, Green Mountains Review, Gulf Stream, Hayden's Ferry Review, Horsethief, iO: New American Poetry, La Petite Zine, Literary Imagination, The Literary Review, Massachusetts Review, The New Guard, New Ohio Review, North American Review, Pleiades, Ploughshares, Prime Number, Salamander, Salt Hill, The Sun, Water~Stone Review, West Branch, The Windsor Review,* and *Word Riot.*

A handful of these poems also appeared in the chapbook, *The Imaginary City* (Organic Weapon Arts, 2012).

MICHAEL BAZZETT is a poet and teacher. His debut collection, *You Must Remember This*, received the 2014 Lindquist & Vennum Prize for Poetry from Milkweed Editions. His translation of *The Popul Vuh*, the first English verse version of the Mayan creation epic, is forthcoming from Milkweed, as is *The Interrogation*, another collection of poems. The recipient of a 2017 NEA fellowship in Poetry, he lives in Minneapolis with his wife and two children.